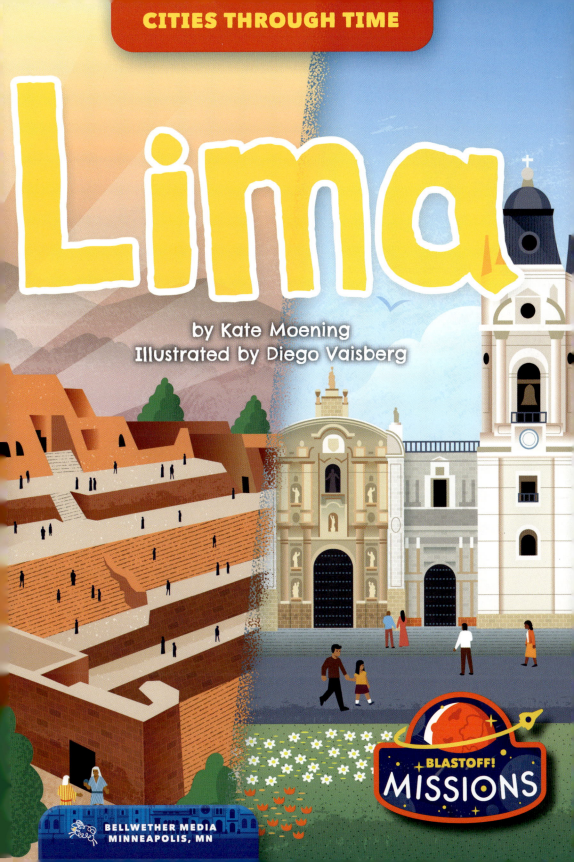

Blastoff! Missions takes you on a learning adventure! Colorful illustrations and exciting narratives highlight cool facts about our world and beyond. Read the mission goals and follow the narrative to gain knowledge, build reading skills, and have fun!

Traditional Nonfiction

Narrative Nonfiction

Blastoff! Universe

MISSION GOALS

> FIND YOUR SIGHT WORDS IN THE BOOK.

> LEARN ABOUT DIFFERENT PERIODS IN LIMA'S HISTORY.

> LEARN ABOUT DIFFERENT GROUPS THAT HAVE CONTROLLED LIMA.

This edition first published in 2025 by Bellwether Media, Inc.

No part of this publication may be reproduced in whole or in part without written permission of the publisher. For information regarding permission, write to Bellwether Media, Inc., Attention: Permissions Department, 6012 Blue Circle Drive, Minnetonka, MN 55343.

Library of Congress Cataloging-in-Publication Data

LC record for Lima available at: https://lccn.loc.gov/2024046806

Text copyright © 2025 by Bellwether Media, Inc. BLASTOFF! MISSIONS and associated logos are trademarks and/or registered trademarks of Bellwether Media, Inc.

Editor: Christina Leaf   Designer: Laura Sowers

Printed in the United States of America, North Mankato, MN.

This is **Blastoff Jimmy**! He is here to help you on your mission and share fun facts along the way!

Table of Contents

Welcome to Lima!	**4**
The Great Temples	**6**
Spanish Rule	**10**
A Free Peru	**14**
The City Today	**20**
Glossary	**22**
To Learn More	**23**
Beyond the Mission	**24**
Index	**24**

Welcome to Lima!

We've arrived in Lima, Peru! Over 11 million people live in this coastal city.

Lima is one of South America's biggest cities. Let's explore its past!

The Great Temples

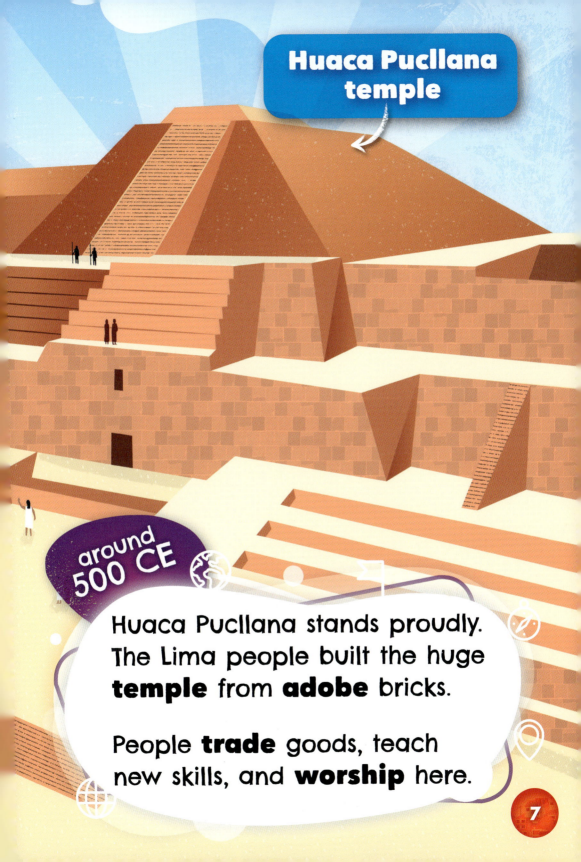

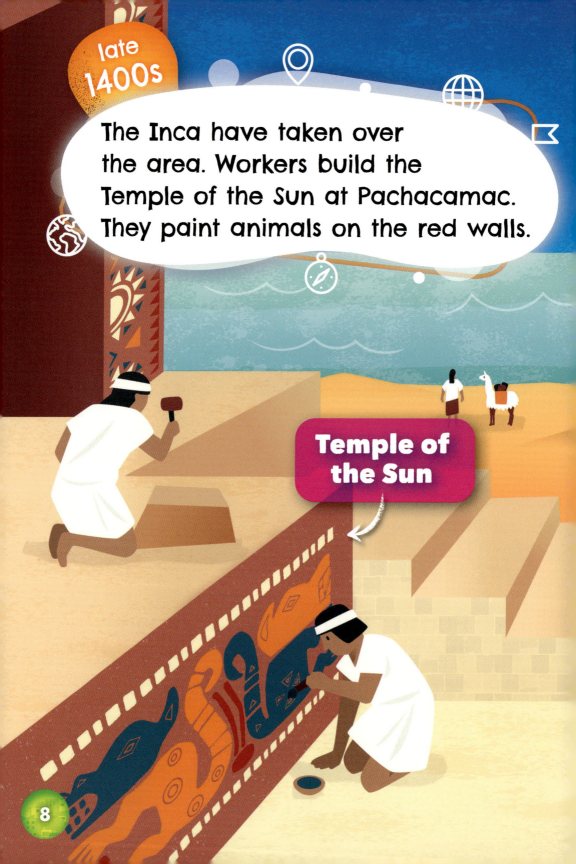

▶ JIMMY SAYS ◀

The new city was built on the coast. This made it easy to send ships back to Spain.

1746

A strong **earthquake** has shaken the city. A big wave crashed over it, too. The capital has been destroyed.

mid-1900s

Lima is growing fast! Over two million people have moved here.

People build **shanties** around the city. The city spreads across many miles.

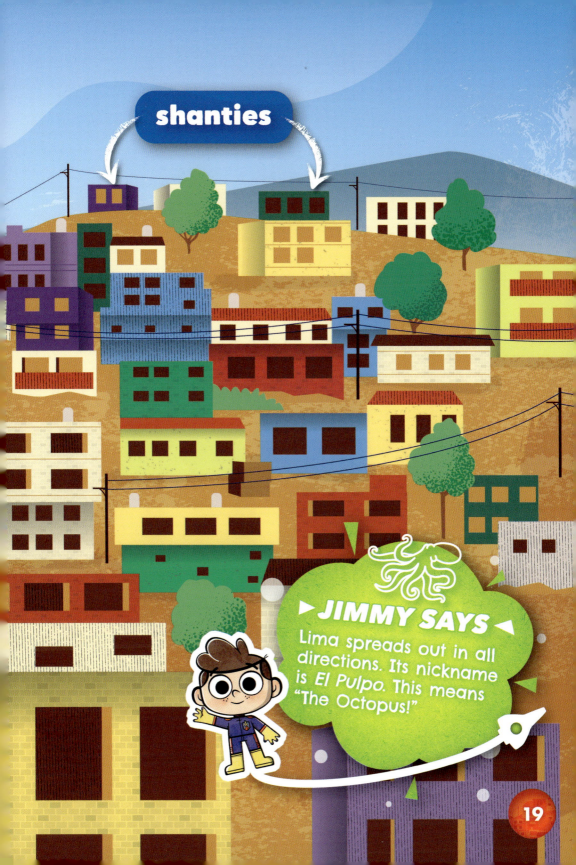

The City Today

today

Lima is a busy place! People visit tall new buildings and old Spanish **plazas**. They shop at Lima's big markets.

Lima has centuries of history!

Lima Timeline

around 500 CE: The Lima people build Huaca Pucllana

late 1400s: The Inca build the Temple of the Sun

1535: Francisco Pizarro starts the city that will become Lima

1746: One of the largest earthquakes in Peru's history hits Lima

1821: Peru claims independence from Spain

1881: The Chilean army occupies Lima and burns down the National Library

mid-1900s: Lima's population grows quickly with over two million new people

Lima, Peru

Glossary

adobe–a building material made of sun-dried earth and straw

earthquake–a sudden movement of the earth's crust

empire–a government with one ruler that rules over a large number of other places and people

occupy–to control using military power

plazas–public squares in cities or towns

port–a place where ships load and unload their containers

shanties–simple buildings or homes, often poorly built

temple–a building used for worship

trade–to buy and sell

worship–to honor something through praying or religion

To Learn More

AT THE LIBRARY

Andrews, Elizabeth. *The Inca*. Minneapolis, Minn.: DiscoverRoo, 2023.

Bjorklund, Ruth, and Sloane Gould. *Peru*. New York, N.Y.: Cavendish Square Publishing, 2023.

Davies, Monika. *Peru*. Minneapolis, Minn.: Bellwether Media, 2024.

ON THE WEB

FACTSURFER

Factsurfer.com gives you a safe, fun way to find more information.

1. Go to www.factsurfer.com.

2. Enter "Lima" into the search box and click 🔍.

3. Select your book cover to see a list of related content.

BEYOND THE MISSION

> WHAT FACT FROM THE BOOK DID YOU THINK WAS THE MOST INTERESTING?

> WHAT ANIMALS WOULD YOU PAINT ON THE TEMPLE OF THE SUN? WHY?

> HOW DO YOU THINK LIMA'S PORT HELPED THE CITY GROW?

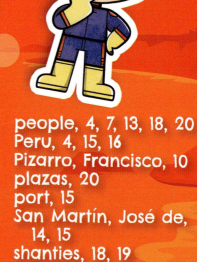

Index

capital, 12
Chilean army, 16, 17
City of the Kings, 10
earthquake, 12
Huaca Pucllana temple, 7
Inca, 8, 10
independence, 15
Lima people, 7
markets, 20
National Library, 16
nickname, 19
Pachacamac, 8
people, 4, 7, 13, 18, 20
Peru, 4, 15, 16
Pizarro, Francisco, 10
plazas, 20
port, 15
San Martín, José de, 14, 15
shanties, 18, 19
South America, 5
Spain, 10, 11, 15, 20
Temple of the Sun, 8, 9
timeline, 21
trade, 7